A TRUE BOOK

North America

LIBBY KOPONEN

Children's Press®
An Imprint of Scholastic Inc.
New York   Toronto   London   Auckland   Sydney
Mexico City   New Delhi   Hong Kong
Danbury, Connecticut

Content Consultant
Jean-Paul Rodrigue, Ph.D.
Associate Professor
Dept. of Economics & Geography
Hofstra University
Hempstead, NY

Library of Congress Cataloging-in-Publication Data

Koponen, Libby.
  North America / by Libby Koponen.
       p. cm. -- (A true book)
  Includes index.
     ISBN-13: 978-0-531-16868-4 (lib. bdg.)
              978-0-531-21830-3 (pbk.)
     ISBN-10: 0-531-16868-9 (lib. bdg.)
              0-531-21830-9 (pbk.)

  1. North America--Juvenile literature. I. Title. II. Series.

  E38.5.K67 2008
  970--dc22

2007048087

Produced by Weldon Owen Education Inc.

©2009 Scholastic Inc.

7 8 9 10 R 18 17 16 15 14

Find the Truth!

Everything you are about to read is true *except* for one of the sentences on this page.

Which one is **TRUE**?

T or F   The Spanish were the first Europeans to explore North America.

T or F   One ancient pyramid in Central America was also a calendar.

Find the answers in this book.

Contents

THE BIG TRUTH!

Bananas are curved because they grow against the pull of gravity.

The Grand Canyon, in western Arizona, is 277 miles (446 kilometers) long. Visitors from all over the world explore its depths. In some places, the canyon is one mile from rim to base.

CHAPTER 1

Continent of Contrasts

← Artifacts 12,000 years old have been discovered in the canyon.

North America's regions are extremely varied. In the far north is the icy Arctic. There the sun shines for only a few hours a day all winter. In the hot western desert, you can cook an egg in the sand. In the south, rain forests host thousands of kinds of plants and animals. On the central plains, grasslands stretch for hundreds of miles. The continent also has farmlands, wetlands, and woodlands. There are 23 countries in North America.

The Far North

North America has more land inside the Arctic Circle than does any other continent. The northern parts of Alaska, Canada, and Greenland are there. In the Arctic, the land is covered by a treeless plain called the tundra. In winter, the land is frozen. The sun comes out for only a few hours each day. Even some of the ocean freezes. In summer, the sun shines for twenty hours a day. Giant cabbages, tiny arctic flowers, and many other plants spring up and transform the land. South of the tundra, a forest stretches across most of Canada.

Greenland is part of North America. However, it belongs to Denmark, which is in Europe.

North America

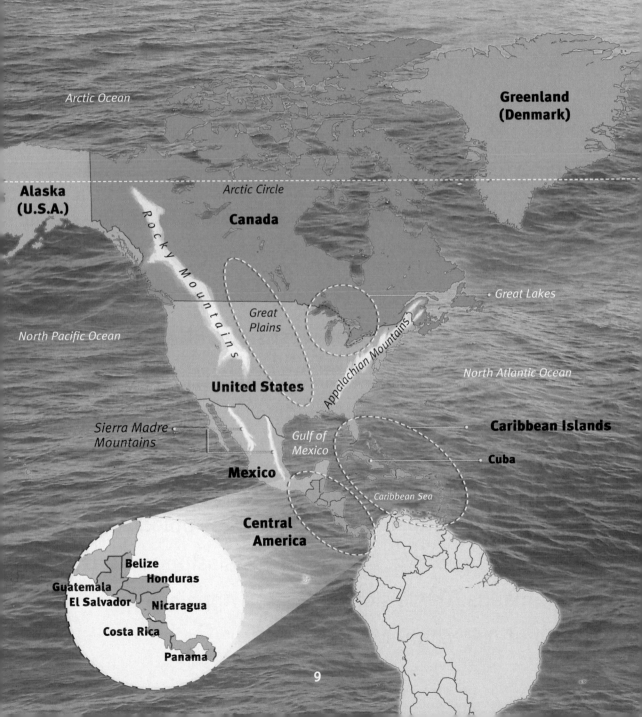

Arctic Ocean

**Greenland
(Denmark)**

**Alaska
(U.S.A.)**

Arctic Circle

Canada

Great Lakes

Rocky Mountains

Great
Plains

North Pacific Ocean

Appalachian Mountains

North Atlantic Ocean

United States

Sierra Madre
Mountains

Gulf of
Mexico

Caribbean Islands

Cuba

Mexico

Caribbean Sea

**Central
America**

Belize
Honduras

Guatemala
El Salvador   **Nicaragua**

Costa Rica

Panama

A ridge in the western mountains divides water flow on the continent. This ridge is called the Continental Divide. West of it, all rivers flow into the Pacific Ocean. East of it, rivers flow into the Gulf of Mexico or the Atlantic Ocean.

Mountains, Deserts, and Rivers

Mountains run down the west side of North America, from Canada to Mexico. In Mexico, they are known as the Sierra Madre. They are called the Rocky Mountains in Canada and the United States. East of the Rockies, plains and prairies stretch aross the continent. Near the Mississippi River, the land slopes down. East of the Mississippi are **fertile** farmlands. These slope up to the Appalachian (ap-uh-LAY-chun) Mountains.

Waterways

Much of the southwest of the continent is desert. Two of the largest cities in the world, Los Angeles and Mexico City, are built in this desert. Both cities get their water from the surrounding mountains. The Los Angeles **aqueduct** system was begun in the early 1900s. It brings water from rivers hundreds of miles away to the city and the farmlands around it.

Mexico and Central America

Mexico is a mountainous country, with fertile valleys and barren deserts. Mexico City has more people than any other city in North America. It was built on top of the ancient **Aztec** capital. The ruins of an Aztec temple were discovered during the building of the city's modern subway system.

Central America is between Mexico and South America, to Mexico's southeast. It is made up of seven small countries. They lie between the Atlantic and Pacific oceans. They have tropical rain forests, beaches, mountains, and farmlands.

Arenal Volcano in Costa Rica is one of the most active volcanoes in the world. On some days, it blows several times in one hour!

Dominican Republic, Caribbean

Island Nations

There are thousands of islands in the Caribbean
Sea. Most of them are completely uninhabited,
even today. Seven are small island nations. A few
are still part of European countries. Some have
volcanoes. All have tropical climates and are
occasionally hit by hurricanes.

Forces of Nature

The power of nature can be overwhelming. It can inspire both wonder and fear. Niagara Falls is one of the great natural wonders of the world. Water from four of the Great Lakes flows over the falls.

Forces of Good

Nature brings many benefits to people. Both Canada and the United States use the water power of the Niagara River to produce electricity. Wind power—when it is not a hurricane or tornado—is another important source of power. Both floods and volcanic eruptions can produce some of the most fertile farmland in the world.

Forces of Destruction

Nature's power can also be destructive. Floods, hurricanes, and blizzards are a few of the more familiar natural disasters. From volcanoes to tornadoes, from mud slides to forest fires—North America experiences every kind of natural disaster, including tsunamis**!**

Polar bears have black skin
and transparent fur. This helps
them absorb heat from the sun.

CHAPTER 2

Wonderful Wildlife

Wild animals of all kinds live in North America. However, their living space has been reduced by loss of forest, of farmland, and of wetland. Animals have reacted to this crowding in unpredictable ways. In some places, animals have become pests. Deer eat people's gardens. Bears and raccoons raid trashcans. However, many animals have learned to cope in ways that go unnoticed by most of us.

The musk ox of the Arctic plains has the longest body hair of any mammal.

Arctic Adaptations

The animals of the Arctic have adapted to life in their icy environment. The arctic ground squirrel sleeps in a den through the winter. Polar bears, walruses, and seals have a thick layer of fat to keep them warm. Musk oxen have two coats of hair. Caribou (KA-ri-boo) have wide hooves for walking on snow. In fact, *caribou* comes from *qalipur*. This is a Native American word meaning "snow shoveler."

Both male and female caribou have antlers. When caribou are tamed, as in Greenland, they are called reindeer.

Blue morpho butterflies are found in Central America. They can measure six inches (15 centimeters) across.

Blue morpho butterflies drink the juice of fermented fruit. They then wobble when they try to fly.

Warm-Weather Creatures

The tropics are home to thousands of animals. North America's largest cat, the jaguar, lives in the rain forest. The harpy eagles there are so big that they can eat monkeys! Caribbean waters support coral reefs, dolphins, and colorful fish. Humpback whales spend winters there. In the middle part of the continent live bears, beavers, foxes, wolves, and many other animals.

Native Americans of the Northwest make totem poles to honor their ancestors.

CHAPTER 3

Looking Back

The eagle was often used as a crest on totem poles.

The first humans in North America walked there from Asia at least 15,000 years ago. They probably crossed on a land bridge that once rose above the Bering Sea. These people and their **descendants** became the first Native Americans. Gradually, they spread out over the whole continent.

The **Inuit** kayaked from Asia to Alaska about 4,000 years ago. They spread across northern Canada to Greenland. Their descendants live in these regions today.

Native Americans and Europeans

By the time Europeans landed in North America, millions of people lived there. In the north, they lived in various tribes with distinct languages and customs. The **Vikings** were the first Europeans to arrive. They sailed from Norway to Canada in around 1000 A.D. The Spanish, French, and English came over about five hundred years later. Diseases that had been unknown in America arrived with them. Millions of Native Americans died.

The Vikings established permanent settlements in Canada. This reconstruction was built on remains of a Viking village discovered in Newfoundland.

Settlements Expand

Beginning in the 1500s, Europeans came to North America in greater numbers. The Spanish settled Florida and California. The English first settled an island off the coast of Virginia in 1607. In 1609, the Dutch landed in what is now New York City.

By the early 1700s, the English and other Europeans had settled all along the east coast. Enslaved Africans were put to work to support these settlements. The settlers traded manufactured goods and weapons with Native American tribes. They also learned from them how to live on the land. But more often, the newcomers and the Native Americans came into conflict with each other. Eventually, the Native Americans were pushed off their tribal lands. They were forced to move west or onto reservations.

The Move West

The East became more crowded. So settlers from Europe and the east coast moved west in covered wagons. The Plains tribes fought against being forced from their lands. Eventually, though, the Plains groups also had to move onto reservations. Many died of diseases. Almost all lost their way of life. Some tribes had relied on the buffalo for nearly all of their needs. The settlers hunted the buffalo almost to extinction.

For protection, many settlers traveled in groups, called wagon trains.

All immigrants underwent health checks on Ellis Island.

Wave of New Immigrants

In the late 1800s, millions more immigrants entered the United States. Like the earlier settlers, they were looking for a fresh start. People came from all over the world, especially from Western Europe. Cities became crowded with new arrivals. Many of these immigrants faced poverty and **prejudice**. For most groups, each new generation blended more easily into the U.S. "melting pot."

Prairie Grasses and Farms

The Great Plains settlers plowed up prairie grasses to plant crops. Then, in the 1930s, there was a long drought. The crops were not tough enough to survive the dry spell. The land turned to dust. Thousands of families left their farms to seek work elsewhere. The so-called Dust Bowl was part of a period of widespread hardship. This period was known as the Great Depression. During this time, U.S. immigration nearly stopped altogether.

Without native grasses to hold down the soil, it blew away in the dry wind.

Mexico

The Spanish arrived in Mexico in 1519. They quickly conquered the Aztec empire, which had ruled since 1427. For nearly 300 years, Spain continued to rule Mexico. Then, in 1810, a priest named Father Hidalgo inspired the people to rise up in revolt. After a ten-year war, Mexico gained its independence in 1821.

Mexicans have big celebrations every year on their Independence Day, September 16.

Central America

The native peoples of Central America did not live in small tribes like those to their north. Large numbers of them had the same rulers, laws, and language. One group, the **Maya**, were brilliant astronomers, weavers, and potters. When Spain took control of Central America, it overpowered the native cultures. Most Central American nations won independence from Spain in the 1830s. In 1903, the United States helped Panama gain its independence. In return, it got to build and control the Panama Canal.

Settlers Time Line

2000 B.C.
The Inuit kayak to North America.

1000 A.D.
The Vikings sail to North America.

The Caribbean Islands

The Spanish were the first to establish colonies in the Caribbean. In the 1600s, other European powers followed. They grew tobacco and sugar cane on huge plantations using slave labor.

Haiti was a colony of France. In 1804, it won its independence. Haiti is the second-oldest independent country in North America.

About half of the Caribbean islands still belong to European countries.

1500s
Europeans sail to North America. Spanish settle Florida and California.

1600s
English and French settle in the east.

CHAPTER 4

The People

North America has only five percent of the world's people. However, it has 16 percent of its land.

Nearly 500 million people live in North America. In Central America, many are of Mayan descent. Elsewhere, too, some are descended from Native Americans. However, most are descended from Europeans, Africans, or Asians. People from every country in the world live in North America. It is a popular destination for people wanting a fresh start.

Much of Quebec City's old town is built in a French style.

Canada

The British took over the French colonies in Canada in 1763. Today, most Canadians have British **ancestors**. However, French culture has survived. About one-fifth of Canadians have French ancestors. Most of these live in the province of Quebec. In 1969, French became Canada's second official language. Since the 1970s, most Canadian children have learned French at school.

The United States

About 69 percent of the people in the United States are descended from Europeans. African Americans make up about 12 percent of the population. The rest of the population is a mix. Native Spanish-speakers now make up 13 percent of the population. Spanish is the most widely spoken language in the United States after English.

Queens, in New York City, is the most ethnically diverse county in the world.

Mexico

When Mexico was a colony of Spain, the Spanish were the ruling class. Gradually, the Spanish mixed with the native peoples. People with both Spanish and native ancestors are known as mestizos. Today, most Mexicans are mestizos and speak Spanish. However, some speak native languages, such as Quiché and Zapotec.

Sun Snake

The Maya built the Pyramid of Kukulkán at Chichén Itzá in about 800 A.D. It is a kind of calendar. There are four sides, with 91 steps each. So, with the top step, there are 365 steps. That is one for each day of the calendar year.

Kukulkán, or "plumed serpent," is named for the shadow cast by the sun twice a year. On the spring and fall **equinoxes**, a serpent appears to be slithering headfirst down the steps of the pyramid.

Serpent's head

The Southern Regions

About 2,000 years ago, the Maya people spread from Mexico into Central America. Today, many Guatemalans still live in small farming villages, the way their Mayan ancestors did. The people in Honduras, Nicaragua, and El Salvador are largely mestizo. On the Atlantic coast of Nicaragua and in Panama, many people have African and Caribbean ancestors. Most Costa Ricans have European ancestors.

In the Caribbean islands, most people are descendants of Africans. Africans were brought to the islands to work on plantations. The islands have a broad mix of cultures, including European and Asian. Dozens of languages are spoken. You can hear French **Creole**, Spanish, Dutch, Hindi, and English, to name several.

St. Martin, in the Caribbean, belongs to France. French is the official language. However, many people speak Creole among themselves.

Many people in Central America grow and trade the same kinds of crops their ancestors have for generations.

CHAPTER 5

Then and Now

The Zuni of New Mexico carve animal figures called fetishes.

North America today must honor the past and welcome the future. There are places on the continent where people live much as they did hundreds of years ago. There are also huge, modern cities. There is great wealth and extreme poverty. The challenge now is to improve people's lives while respecting diverse cultures and traditions.

Producers and Suppliers

Canada and the United States are among the world's top producers of manufactured goods and food supplies. They have many natural resources, such as minerals and natural gas. They also produce nearly half of the world's grain exports.

Mexico recently made a special agreement with the United States and Canada. It promotes more trade among the three countries. The effects have been mixed. Half the population of Mexico still lives in poverty.

Some Central American goods are sold through fair trade organizations.

Some farmers grow coffee slowly in the shade. This is better for the soil and the environment.

Living off the Land

Many countries in Central America and the Caribbean islands are among the least developed in the world. In the countries that have stable governments, conditions are improving. More and more people work in service industries, such as in restaurants and hotels. **Ecotourism** is also growing. Central America remains a leading exporter of coffee and bananas.

Looking Ahead

Today, more people than ever are moving around the globe. The mix of cultures in North America is growing richer every day. Most people now settle in or near big cities. Meanwhile, rural areas are losing population. Communities are facing change. But immigrants continue to arrive, hoping to make new, better lives in North America. ★

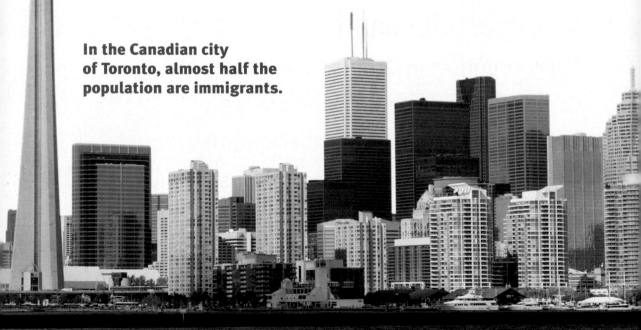

In the Canadian city of Toronto, almost half the population are immigrants.

True Statistics

Size of continent: About 9,400,000 square miles (24,345,888 square kilometers)

Population of continent: About 515,000,000

Largest lake: Lake Superior — 31,820 square miles (82,413 square kilometers)

Number of independent countries: 23

Hottest place: Death Valley, CA — 134°F (56.7°C)

Largest turtle: Leatherback — about 1,000 pounds (454 kilograms)

Smallest bird: Bee hummingbird — about .06 ounce (1.8 grams)

Did you find the truth?

F The Spanish were the first Europeans to explore North America.

T One ancient pyramid in Central America was also a calendar.

43

Resources

Books

Armstrong, Jennifer. *The American Story*. New York: Knopf Publishing, 2006.

Cox, Caroline and Albala, Ken. *Opening Up North America, 1497–1800* (Discovery & Exploration). New York: Facts on File, 2005.

Fowler, Allan. *North America* (Rookie Read-About Geography*)*. New York: Children's Press, 2001.

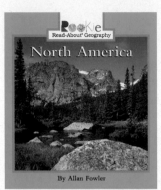

Johnston, Lissa. *A Brief Political and Geographic History of North America: Where Are New France, New Netherland, and New Sweden?* (Places in Time) Hockessin, DE: Mitchell Lane Publishers, 2007.

Mara, Wil. *The Seven Continents* (Rookie Read-About Geography). New York: Children's Press, 2005.

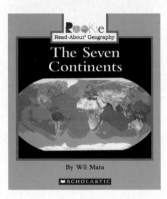

Meachen Rau, Dana. *North America* (Continents). Mankato, MN: The Child's World, 2003.

Storey Publishing. *Wild Animals of North America*. North Adams, MA, 2006.

Organizations and Web Sites

The Great Lakes for Kids
www.on.ec.gc.ca/greatlakeskids
Videos, games, and cartoons teach all
about the importance of the Great Lakes.

National Park Service for Kids
www.nps.gov/webrangers
Try games, quizzes, and other activities to learn about
the many national parks in the United States.

British Columbia Archives
www.bcarchives.gov.bc.ca/exhibits/timemach/index.htm
Enter a time machine to find out how people lived in Canada
in the past.

Places to Visit

Ellis Island Immigration Museum
National Park Service
New York, NY 10004
(212) 344 0996
www.ellisisland.com
Explore the place where
many people started their
lives in North America.

National Museum of the American Indian
4th St./Independence Ave., S.W.
Washington, DC 20560
(202) 633 1000
www.nmai.si.edu
Discover a huge collection
of artifacts and information
about Native Americans.

Important Words

ancestor (AN-sess-tur) – a family member who died long ago

aqueduct (AK-wuh-duhkt) – a channel constructed to transport water over a long distance

Aztec (AZ-tek) – a civilization that flourished in Mexico for about 300 years, until the arrival of the Spanish in 1519

Creole (KREE-ohl) – a local form of the French language

descendant – one of the children, grandchildren, great-grandchildren, and so on, of a person

ecotourism – tourist activities based on respect for nature

equinox – one of the two days of the year when day and night are equally long all over the world, due to the position of the sun

fertile (FUR-tuhl) – good for growing plants and crops

Inuit (IN-oo-it) – indigenous people of the Arctic north

Maya (MYE-uh) – a civilization that flourished in Mexico and Central America in about 1000 A.D.

prejudice (PREJ-uh-diss) – a fixed, unfair opinion based on race, religion, or another general characteristic

tsunami (tsoo-NAH-mee) – a large wave triggered by an underwater earthquake or volcano

Viking – one of the Scandinavian warriors who invaded European countries between 800 A.D. and 1100 A.D.

Index

Page numbers in **bold** indicate illustrations

About the Author

Libby Koponen is the author of *South America*, another True Book, and *Blow Out the Moon*, a novel based on a true story about an American girl who goes to an English boarding school. Libby has a B.A. in history from Wheaton College and an M.F.A. in writing from Brown University. She has traveled all over the world and ridden horses on every continent except Antarctica. She lives in Mystic, CT.